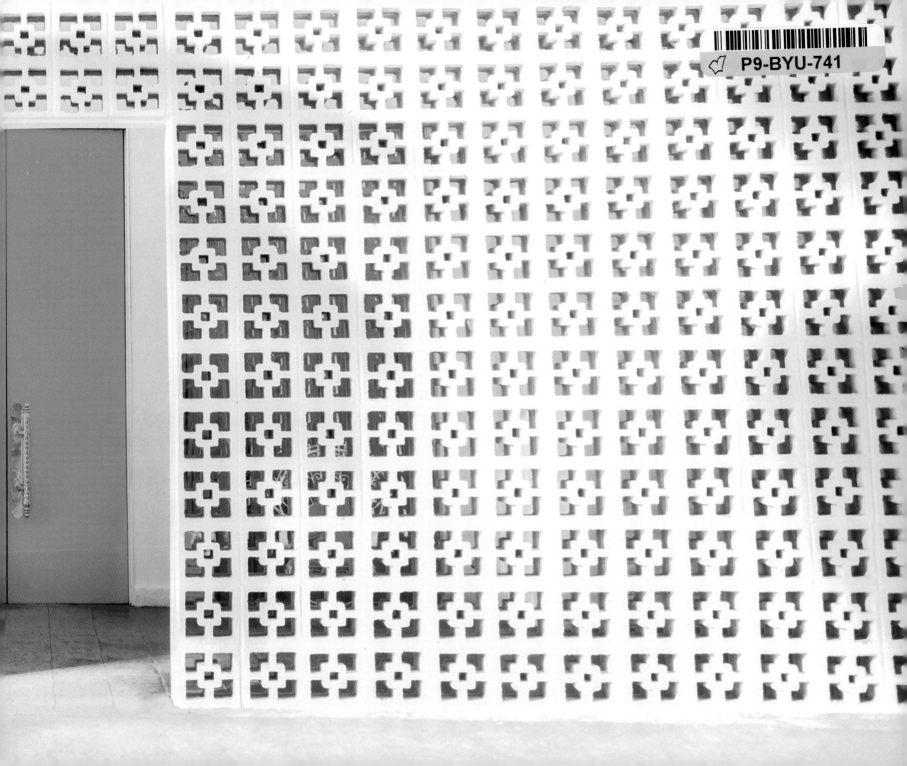

BE OUR GUEST!

Not Your *Ordinary* Vacation

GRAY MALIN

Abrams Books for Young Readers
New York

Welcome to the Parker Hotel. We are excited to have you as our guest!

The hotel is very **ORDINARY.** But we love it here.

I'm Maurice, the concierge. Let me show you around.

Say hello to Mr. Parker, the owner of our hotel. The hotel has been in his family since he was a young **CUB.**

This is our lobby.

All of our guests like to hang out and **MONKEY** around.

First, let's **HOP** over and get a key to your room from Wally at the front desk.

This will be your room during your stay.

Perhaps you'd like to relax and watch some TV?

There's a channel for every guest's **TASTE!**

I've made sure your bed is . . .

EXTRA comfortable.

The pillows are fluffy . . .   and the blankets are cozy.

Look, it's Callie.

She's another guest,
JUST like you!

She's off to our favorite
watering hole.

Would you care to take a swim in our pool?

Peter and Pippa are **ORDINARY** lifeguards, but when they're off-duty they'll show you their diving tricks.

Or you can **COOL OFF** with some other guests at the lemonade stand.

Sometimes Timmy stops by for a sip. He likes to **PROWL** around in the afternoon.

Here at the Parker,
we love to play GAMES.

Do you like tennis or chess?

Hide-
and-
seek?

How about a game of ping-pong?

You'll meet lots of new friends at the Parker.
They're **JUST** like your friends back home.

Look!

I see some balloons.

Do you think there's
going to be a **PARTY?**

Let's
　　follow
　　　　the
　　　　　　balloons . . .

Eliza's **CHARGING** ahead!

Timmy is groomed
and ready to

ROAR!

Our parties
can get a little
WILD!

The lovebirds are total
PARTY ANIMALS.

Pierre the pastry chef has baked us some delicious **TREATS.**

It's party time!
Let's **PIG** out . . .

and go BANANAS!

Mr. Parker takes **PRIDE** in our hotel and its majestic grounds.

He hopes you enjoy your stay and feel like you are part of the **PACK!**

Would you like to be a guest at our **ORDINARY** hotel again?

AUTHOR'S NOTE

The playful grounds of my favorite hotel, the Parker Palm Springs, are a modern-day fantasyland filled with hammocks under towering palm trees, croquet and pétanque courts, vintage umbrellas, and lemonade stands by swimming pools.

This lush atmosphere caused my imagination to run wild, and I began to envision a perfect oasis for my favorite exotic animals—a hotel where you are greeted by a monkey instead of a bellhop, where you can sip lemonade with flamingos, play chess with penguins, and take a dip with a camel!

I visited the hotel on three occasions from 2014 to 2017 to photograph this collection of work, and researched ethical ways of capturing these shots. My team and I worked with an organization that has over thirty years of experience in maintaining the highest safety standards when working with animals in the film and advertising industries. With affection training methods and positive reinforcement, such as verbal praise and tasty rewards, the organization ensured a happy and calm environment for the animals. I was immediately inspired by the mutual respect and trust the animals and their trainers showed one another, and it was clear that they had developed a deep bond of friendship.

Working with animals was full of surprise and awe. I'll never forget the moment a 550-pound lion—whose real name is Felix—marched out of the front doors of the Parker Palm Springs in all of his majesty! Though my favorite memory of all was when Tiny, the baby giraffe, stole a kiss when I was photographing him by the pool.

It was a pleasure to work with each and every one of these *ordinary* animals. They truly made my vision come to life.

—Gray Malin, 2018

To the **ORDINARY** kid in all of us
—G.M.

Thank you to my wonderful staff and
the editors at Abrams who helped bring
the magic of this book to life.

The images in this book were created with the use of
digital photography and minimal editing.

Cataloging-in-Publication Data has been applied for
and may be obtained from the Library of Congress.

ISBN 978-1-4197-2930-0

Printed and bound in U.S.A.
10 9 8 7 6 5 4 3 2

Abrams Books for Young Readers are available at
special discounts when purchased in quantity for
premiums and promotions as well as fundraising
or educational use. Special editions can also be
created to specification. For details, contact
specialsales@abramsbooks.com or the address below.

ABRAMS The Art of Books
195 Broadway, New York, NY 10007
abramsbooks.com